This book
belongs to:

_____

Jewish Holiday Fun For You!

by Barbara Rushkoff

Art by Jack Pollock

Doofus and Moishey Art by Mindy Sparango

Universe

First published in the United States of America in 2004
by UNIVERSE PUBLISHING
A Division of Rizzoli International Publications, Inc.
300 Park Avenue South
New York, NY 10010
www.rizzoliusa.com

© 2003 by Barbara Rushkoff

2004 2005 2006 2007/ 10 9 8 7 6 5 4 3 2 1

Design by Sean Tejaratchi

Printed in Mexico

ISBN: 0-7893-1196-8

Library of Congress Control Number: 2004108274

For Douglas

Introduction

GROWING UP JEWISH in a predominantly non-Jewish area wasn't a big deal. Well, until Christmas. That's when the neighborhood kids wanted to know what was up with the lame plastic lamp in our window. As I tried to juice up the story about the miracle of Hanukkah (which nobody was buying anyway), I was always met with the same bottom line: "So, why don't you guys have a tree?"

And no matter how many times I said "because we're Jewish," they didn't really get it. Jews in my 'hood were an enigma. We were thought of as peculiar people with strange holiday foods; people who have something against blinking Santas and electric reindeer. What really got me was how our holidays occurred at roughly the same times during the year, but they couldn't have been more different. They had chocolate bunnies, candy canes, and tasty communion wafers. We had bitter herbs, nasty fruit rings, and gefilte fish in a glass jar. I was confused.

As I got older, it didn't get any better. I frequently met bona fide grown-ups who had no idea what Jews do on Christmas. I was cautiously asked about my whereabouts on December 25th, as if that was the day I set aside to do human sacrifice. After exploding into a tirade about how Jews don't celebrate Christmas because "we're not Christian" (duh), I would explain that sometimes I did laundry or met with friends, but most times you could find me laying face down on my bed wishing that they'd stop running the creepy movie "A Christmas Carol." That usually shut them up.

However, I didn't want to be the angry Jewess who appears on Christmas to curse out the people who put cardboard elves on my desk. So instead of taking out my rage on clueless co-workers with tinsel fixations, I started in on the truly wrath worthy—fellow Jews who felt the need for something called a Hanukkah bush. I pointed out that Jews may not get a tree (or cheeky elves that want to become dentists), but we have something better. We get to light menorah candles. Which means we get to play with fire. Sure, throwing tinsel on a tree is fun, but it's just not FIRE.

Yes, US GUYS have our own holidays with our own traditions (which sometimes include fun activities like burning things). We also have righteous holidays like Shavuot. This holiday celebrates feminism by telling the story of Ruth, who redeemed her family's land in a time when ladies were not given their rightly props. Then there's Shabbat, the weekly holiday where women become momentary priestesses while they light the candles. And what about Purim, aka the Jewish Halloween? The narrative of this holiday is a miniseries in the making. The story has juicy roles for women, fun-to-watch bad guys, ethnic pride, and even a beheading. What's more fun than THAT?

Once I got my cranium around each holiday and uncovered the so-called mystifying roots, I wanted everyone to know the real deal. But instead of going around with a bible in my hand pointing out scripture, I decided to write a book (you're soaking in it). I've tried to retell each holiday in a modern context, sometimes in outdated rap language, sometimes in botched Yiddish, but always with humor and plenty of facts. C'mon, who doesn't want the 411 on Simchat Torah courtesy of characters named Doofus and Moishey?

Jewish holidays are not unsolvable mysteries (unless you're counting Tu Bishvat, the one where you plant trees in Israel and then never, ever hear about them again). Some are joyous, some have more symbolism than a gothic novel, and some are just about suffering (and I'm not even talking about the food involved). Mostly they're fascinating accounts that can sometimes appear as wacky and unusual. And that's something we Jews should be proud of and that non-Jews should admire—stinky gefilte fish and all.

I hope these stories entertain and make you laugh. And if you learn something in the process, it wouldn't kill you, either. Mostly this book is for anyone who has ever lived through the holidays or hopes to in the future. But it's also for anyone who wants to crack the mystery of Jewish holidays. So have fun, laugh, and learn—and then never ask us again what us guys do on Christmas!

THE HIGH HOLY DAYS are, like, the biggest test of your life, an exam that you can't study for because you are being graded on your efforts of the past year. Talk about the mother of cumulative effects. And if you flunk, well, let's just say you don't get to do a make-up. EVER AGAIN.

But what if you're not good at fasting or standing up for a long time in services or forgiving people who got you really mad? Is there such a thing as flunking the High Holy Days? Not really. It's all about setting the record straight, clearing the slate, and learning to be a better person.

Which if you think about it is so much easier than any SAT test you'll ever take.

The High Holidays

Do not turn to any other section in the test.

If you finish before time is called, you may correct your work using the guide below.

STOP

The serious ones about fasting and making up with the horrible people who made you mad the last year.

9

Rosh Hashanah and Yom Kippur – The High Holy Days

Instructions for High Holy Days Reading Comprehension: Rosh Hashanah is indeed the Jewish New Year, but it is not celebrated like the New Year's Day that comes around every January 1st. There are no Dick Clark Rockin' New Year's television specials, nor are there months of planning what you are going to wear on that fateful night when dinners double in price and all of sudden it becomes all too important where you'll be precisely at midnight. Also, there is no grown man dressed up as a Baby New Year—but that's not necessarily a bad thing.

Rosh Hashanah is a celebration marking the start of a brand new year, and celebrated by attending long holiday services in a stifling, hot room that smells like old ladies' perfume. It's a holiday of contemplation and standing on your feet too much. Its sister holiday, Yom Kippur, comes soon after and is the day to think of past sins. You get a clean slate by fasting for an entire day. That means not even a drop of water—or vodka!

It's the time of year to make up with enemies (even if they are horrible rotten bastards and you still hate them), to right wrongs (even if you were right in the first place), and to generally be as nice as you should have been all year (next year, in Jerusalem?). So, on your marks—ready, set, atone!

Questions 1-8 are based on the following passage.

Passage 1

My mother invited our neighbors over on the eve of Rosh Hashanah to informally welcome the New Year. There was only one other Jewish family on the block, the Finkelsteins, but they didn't come. My mother said they were "unsociable." However, their daughter, Phyllis, showed up. She was wearing one of her plastic copper wigs (the one with marcel waves). Backwards.

"Happy Rosh Hashanah," she said, peeking her entire head into our house.

Phyllis had on a scooter skirt with a bathing suit top, beaten-up Keds, and her grandmother's green crocheted shawl. She looked like Marcia Brady on the crack pipe.

I grabbed my sister and the three of us got some apples and honey, the traditional foods of the holiday, to conjure up a sweet new year. As Phyllis gobbled up two whole apples, she asked if she could come with us to services the next day. I was glad for her company because services could be pretty boring. Maybe she'd bring us wigs to wear!

And so at 8:58 the next morning, there was Phyllis sitting on our porch with a big smile. Attending services was sort of somber, but Phyllis was a bright light, especially in her orange Day-Glo jumper and tie-dyed sneakers

GO ON TO THE NEXT PAGE ⟩

with her Hebrew name written in black marker. Phyllis told me that G-d hears you better if you're standing up, so it's best to wear comfortable shoes. I pondered this as I adjusted the Band-Aid on my new shiny patent leather kicks.

Phyllis had a big suede-fringed bag with her. Inside was sustenance for the long service: a four-pack of wintergreen Lifesavers, watermelon lip-gloss and pretzels. Jews can indeed eat on Rosh Hashanah. It just usually isn't done *during* services.

Luckily, my parents wouldn't be around to chaperone us, as they were ensconced in the fancy main room called the Sanctuary. It was not a Goth club where everyone showed up in black lipstick and white pancake makeup. However, it was a kind of club, considering that annual dues must be paid in order to get a seat during this season. For those who didn't pay the high premium, there was a room called the Auditorium for low-budget praying.

It was a wood-paneled cavern that smelled vaguely of Halston perfume, kasha, and guilt. When the room wasn't being used for religious purposes, it was frequently turned into alternative ways for the synagogue to make money, like a Las Vegas night or a square dancing party.

Phyllis made a crack about skipping-to-her-lou during particularly boring parts of the service and I secretly hoped that she'd get up and sashay herself onto the bimah. But that's not what Rosh Hashanah is really about. It's the time to make up with friends, settle all arguments, and channel your inner menschette. I thought about all the people I had fought with the past year and how bad I'd been (*very* bad, I was even being bad at synagogue!) and how I could be a better person. Granted, it's hard to concentrate when your mouth is filled with pretzels, but I tried as best I could.

1. What does one customarily eat on Rosh Hashanah?
(A) Nothing, it's a fasting holiday
(B) Two all beef patties, special sauce, lettuce, cheese, pickles, and onions, on a sesame seed bun
(C) Apples and honey
(D) Halston perfume

2. What secular holiday most resembles Rosh Hashanah?
(A) Labor Day
(B) All Saints' Day
(C) Kwanzaa
(D) New Year's Day

3. What room do Goth bands perform in during the High Holy Days?
(A) The Auditorium
(B) The Sanctuary
(C) Goth bands only come out at Purim
(D) None of the above

GO ON TO THE NEXT PAGE

4. How far in advance should you be extra nice to Aunt Gussie in order for her to let you sit in her fancy paid seats?

    (A) Three months
    (B) Two weeks
    (C) The day before Rosh Hashanah
    (D) You should always be nice to Aunt Gussie

5. What's a tuchis?
    (A) A flank steak
    (B) Your boss
    (C) A brand of pretzels
    (D) You're sitting on it

6. How does one channel one's inner menschette?
    (A) By being nice all the time, even to people who don't deserve it
    (B) By being nice all the time, only to people who deserve it
    (C) Through a special tube implanted near your ear
    (D) With a VCR

7. ROSH HASHANAH: JUDAISM::
    (A) chocolate bunny: Easter
    (B) birthday: Jehovah's Witness
    (C) Halloween: paganism
    (D) Good Friday: Passover

8. AUDITORIUM: SANCTUARY::
    (A) orchestra seats: nosebleed section
    (B) toy car: Mercedes
    (C) Phyllis: the congregation
    (D) Rhoda Morgenstern: Mary Richards

Questions 9-16 are based on the following passage.

Passage 2

    It was still blazing hot out but that didn't stop most of the Sisterhood from showcasing their new fall wardrobes on this Rosh Hashanah. We stood on the steps outside of the synagogue during a self-imposed break from all the praying to gaze at the ersatz fashion parade.

    "Look at Mrs. Finer's thigh-high boots!" I yelled. "She looks like a lady wrestler who's ready to rumble!"

    "Forget her boots, check out her schnozz job," piped in Phyllis.

    "Wait, look at her husband. Why is he wearing a dead animal on his head?" shrieked my sister.

    I felt a little bad about our comments, but maybe that was because we were making them too loudly. We garnered some attention from one synagogue staffer, who came over wearing quite the stink-eye. I think he used to be our dentist but I couldn't be sure. People look different in yarmulkes.

    "You girls should be inside instead of committing Lashon ha'Ra out here."

GO ON TO THE NEXT PAGE >

The three of us hung our heads. We were so busted. The term Lashon ha'Ra means "bad tongue" (not to be confused with poor-quality deli meat). There are three degrees of Lashon ha'Ra and I think we committed all of them that day. The first is *trivial,* because it is non-defamatory gossip of other people's lives. The second is formally called *Lashon Ha-Ra* and can be characterized as negative, though truthful information about people. The third level is *Motzi Shem Ra* and is the most damaging because it is the spreading of malicious rumors that turn out to be totally untrue. "All of the phases of Lashon ha'Ra are naughty, and doing it on the High Holy Days is doubly bad," said the dentist who was now shuffling us back into the synagogue with a questionable sweeping motion of his hand on our backsides.

Seated on a fold out chair in the auditorium, bloated on pretzels, I thought about what just transpired. I felt crummy and wanted to talk to Phyllis about it. But when I glanced over and saw her ensemble I found myself thinking of three forms of Lashon ha'Ra to describe it.

The sound of the shofar snapped me out of this stinkin' thinkin'. This special ram's horn is blown like a musical instrument although it does not sound like anything that you'd actually ever want to hear. There are four different notes: tekiah, a three-second sustained note; shevarim, three one-second notes rising in tone; teruah, a series of short, staccato notes; and tekiah gedolah, the final, longest blast. The sho-far's reverberation is a cross between an over-due pregnant cow and unfortunate jazz improvisation. I was getting a headache. Wasn't there some way to make it sound like a top 40 hit?

"Hey, Phyllis, we should get shofars and learn how to play "Gypsies, Tramps and Thieves" on them," I said in earnest.

"No way. That thing is harder to blow than a eunuch," Phyllis replied.

I didn't quite know what she meant, but took it as a discouraging sign and focused on my prayer book instead.

9. Rosh Hashanah often occurs in what month?
(A) February
(B) September
(C) December
(D) That secret 13th month

10. The term for bad-mouthing someone is:
(A) "La Vida Loca"
(B) Latoya Jackson
(C) Lashon ha'Ra
(D) *La Dolce Vita*

11. What are the best words to describe the style of Phyllis Finkelstein's attire?
(A) Shtetl fabulous
(B) Shiksational
(C) Teen vogue
(D) Meshuggeneh retro

GO ON TO THE NEXT PAGE

12. The shofar is:
(A) That new underage bar in midtown
(B) An instrument made from a ram's horn
(C) The rabbi's way of letting you know that it's time to wake up.
(D) That new rapper. ("Yo, representin")

13. Tekiah gedolah sounds like:
(A) Nat King Cole on a good day
(B) Diana Ross on a bad day
(C) Broadway and 42nd Street during rush hour
(D) Your upstairs neighbors when they're "in the mood"

14. What is a eunuch?
(A) That last guy you dated
(B) Meat-flavored candy
(C) An extreme case of a circumcision gone wrong
(D) A drink that contains no alcohol

15. RHINOPLASTY: BOTOX::
(A) old school: new school
(B) surgeon: dermatologist
(C) nudnik: meshuggeneh
(D) cat lady: frozen face

16. GOSSIP: CARRYINGS-ON::
(A) damage: words
(B) stories: telemovies
(C) eating in synagogue: activity
(D) so & so: what's-her-name

Questions 17-24 are based on the following passage.

Passage 3

We hadn't seen Phyllis since we dropped her off on Rosh Hashanah, but ten days later on Yom Kippur there she was again, waiting on the porch for a ride. I had learned to curb my Lashon ha'Ra and almost feel guilty at reporting on her attire that day. But I will anyway: faded prairie dress that dragged on the floor, flip-flops, Minnie Mouse earrings, and a head-scarf like "Rhoda" wears.

"I hope you didn't brush your teeth," were the first words out of Phyllis's mouth.

"Of course I brushed. That's gross."

"Toothpaste counts," said Phyllis. "You broke the fast already."

I refused to believe her. I know that you can't drink a drop of water on Yom Kippur, but brushing your teeth? Unfortunately, by the stench awaiting us in the synagogue, I feared that a lot of people sided with Phyllis on this toothpaste hubbub.

Yom Kippur is the day where G-d decides who will live and who will die that year and so Jews fast to purify themselves of the sins they've built up. The gravity of the situation should have been enough to make me lose my appetite, but that didn't seem to be happening. In fact, I was hungrier than I'd ever been. Kibitzing with Phyllis didn't work either. She didn't have food or wigs with her, and since we

GO ON TO THE NEXT PAGE

had stopped bad-mouthing other people there was nothing else to do anyway.

Thankfully, services ended at one o'clock. Only six more hours until dinner! Phyllis was sent home and my mother told us to go into the house and do whatever we wanted, as long as we remained catatonic and didn't eat. This was the time to meditate on how bad we had been for a whole year. I usually deliberated on what we were going to have for dinner or reminisced about how lucky I was to have once been sick on Yom Kippur. Loophole: the sick and infirm can eat without retribution from G-d. If only I had the flu.

As I was staring at our white wood paneling wondering what it tasted like (I told you that I was hungry), the doorbell rang. It was Phyllis asking my mother if my sister and me could go over to her house. Although Phyllis lived across the street, going to her house was a rare occurrence. Mrs. Finkelstein had strict rules for visiting and if you didn't follow the rules exactly you could *never, ever* play there again.

Think of a cylindrical feminine hygiene product and that starts to explain Mrs. Fawn Finkelstein. Her minimalist house was continuously set to an icy temperature and it was always dark inside. The furniture was beige and boxy and nothing looked comfortable. Also, the window shades were pulled down so tightly that my mother speculated Mrs. Finkelstein might be growing mushrooms in her kitchen.

"We're not allowed upstairs," said Phyllis. "Let's go to the cellar."

Mrs. Finkelstein made the gas-face as we passed on our way downstairs. The rec-room floor was cold with ugly linoleum that smelled of mold, Spaghetti-O's, and oppression. The one saving grace was that Phyllis's dog Randie lived down there. She cuddled up to me as we played board games still in our synagogue dresses. As long as we weren't eating, none of us felt guilty about popping the pop-o-matic bubble on Trouble. I was concentrating on the game as Phyllis nonchalantly dug her hand into Randie's food dish and started eating from it as if it was popcorn.

"Phyllis, what are you doing?" my sister and I screamed in unison.

"It tastes just like iced tea," Phyllis said casually.

"Iced tea comes in a chemical powder that you mix up with water," I said with real know-how. "And besides, it's Yom Kippur."

"This doesn't count as real food."

My sister and I looked at each other in disbelief then acute awareness. Was Phyllis on to something here?

17. What is decided on the Day of Atonement?
(A) Who will faint from hunger
(B) Who will live and who will die
(C) Who will be the first one to implore people in the synagogue to please take a breath mint
(D) All of the above

GO ON TO THE NEXT PAGE ⟶

18. What activities are acceptable on Yom Kippur?

    (A) Stand up. Sit down. Pray. Stand up. Sit down. Pray.

    (B) Guessing who got plastic surgery during synagogue services

    (C) Eating secretly in your room, away from where G-d can see you

    (D) Getting a huge migraine from hunger

19. What thing best describes Mrs. Fawn Finklestein?

    (A) A bubble bath

    (B) A warm hug

    (C) A smiley face button

    (D) A tampon

20. What was Phyllis's reasoning for eating dog food on Yom Kippur?

    (A) Fasting day or not, her dog Randie would be insulted if she didn't eat some hors d'oeuvres.

    (B) It was the pop-o-matic bubble's fault.

    (C) Dog food doesn't count as real food.

    (D) She likes to show off.

21. If someone is insane in the membrane, do they still have to fast on Yom Kippur?

    (A) No, the sick and infirm can chow down as hard as they want to without any worry.

    (B) Yes, they must fast. So what if someone doesn't take his or her anti-psychotic medicine for one lousy day?

    (C) Yes, especially those suffering from psychosomatic illnesses.

    (D) It's an individual choice between all your personalities.

22. Was Phyllis Finkelstein sinning anew as she ate on Yom Kippur or could her behavior be tacked onto last year's sins?

    (A) Eating dog food is almost like punishing yourself, so she could have been canceling out her sins.

    (B) Phyllis meant to atone for last year's sins, and last year's sins only. However, it is best to do so without accruing new sins.

    (C) No matter how you look at it, dog food does not taste like iced tea, so Phyllis can be thought of as insane and, thus, can eat to her heart's (or tail's) content without fear that she is sinning at all.

    (D) Maybe.

23. DOG FOOD: ICED TEA::

    (A) reality: dream world

    (B) mom's meatloaf: indigestion

    (C) hunger: mirage

    (D) kibbles: bits

24. HALITOSIS: YOM KIPPUR SERVICES::

    (A) auditorium: stench

    (B) teeth: enlightenment

    (C) headache: mother

    (D) cramps: prom night

GO ON TO THE NEXT PAGE

Questions 25-32 are based on the following passage.

Passage 4

I know Judaism was intended as an open discussion but I wondered if the question of dog food ever entered into it. I certainly wasn't going to fight with Phyllis about it on Yom Kippur though. I was winning at Trouble and wanted to get back to *that*.

"Don't you get thirsty?" my sister inquired.

"Well," Phyllis paused, as if to deliver so much knowledge all at once that we'd need a moment to process it. "That's the neat thing. You can add tap water to it and it makes it juicy. Try it, you'll liiiiiiike it." She mimicked a favorite commercial of mine to entice me.

My sister had a kibble up to her lips, but I glared at her hard, not so much because I was disgusted but because it was Yom Kippur. Then I looked at Phyllis. She had long flowing hair like an Irish setter. She did have quite the shiny coat, but we couldn't allow our friend to do this any more. We decided to perform an intervention by getting down on all fours and wagging our bottoms while barking in different dog voices.

"What will you do when you start growing a tail?" we asked.

The thing is, if anyone could grow a tail Phyllis could.

After 2.2 seconds, Mrs. Finkelstein summoned us back upstairs. She reminded me of that woman on TV who was always having terrible headache moments.

"I'll give you girls 10 cents each if you leave right now."

My sister and I weren't dummies. We took the money and left.

When we got home my mother was sipping a secret cup of tea. I didn't bother to tell her about the details of our visit across the street because I didn't want to commit Lashon ha'Ra. Miraculously, I hadn't eaten anything all day and wanted to remain as clean as possible. My father was getting ready to go back to synagogue for the end portion of the Yom Kippur service. As usual, as soon as he left my mother pulled out the pot roast for us to eat. But for some reason I wasn't even hungry. However, I did have a giant glass of iced tea.

25. Please select the correct example of *trivial* Lashon ha'Ra:

(A) Fawn Finkelstein's house is always dark.

(B) The Finkelsteins are Amish and they don't use electricity.

(C) Phyllis Finkelstein's house is dark because they belong to a Satanic cult and Satan likes it that way.

(D) Fawn Finkelstein is Satan.

GO ON TO THE NEXT PAGE

26. Please select the correct example of *Lashon Ha-Ra*:

(A) Phyllis Finkelstein has been known to eat dog food.

(B) Phyllis Finkelstein eats dog food on kosher rye bread.

(C) Phyllis Finkelstein forcibly feeds dog food to the neighborhood kids.

(D) Phyllis Finkelstein grew up to write a book entitled *Lose It on the Gravy Train: Drop Ugly Fat The Kibble Way!*

27. Please select the correct example of *Motzi Shem Ra*:

(A) Fawn Finkelstein's house is dark because she is growing "funny" mushrooms that she serves to Phyllis along with dog food.

(B) Phyllis Finkelstein loves dog food and wants to one day grow up to endorse it on television.

(C) The Finkelsteins often bring casseroles made entirely of dog food to their neighbors.

(D) All of the above

28. Was Mrs. Finkelstein performing a mitzvah (good deed) when she paid us to leave her house?

(A) Mitzvahs generally don't count if they're under $100.

(B) No, it is not a mitzvah to drive people from your home.

(C) Considering the source, perhaps for Mrs. Finkelstein, it was a mitzvah.

(D) Spending money on Yom Kippur is forbidden, so it was not a mitzvah.

29. What was Mother doing when we got home from Phyllis's house?

(A) Having an international coffee moment.

(B) Relishing the quiet.

(C) White-knuckling it with a secret cup of tea.

(D) Thinking about starting a neighborhood watch on the Finkelstein home.

30. What was the main point of this Yom Kippur story?

(A) Dog food is bad; money is good.

(B) Eating is bad; sinning is bad.

(C) Cleansing is good; sinning is bad.

(D) Going to Phyllis' house is bad; telling on her is good.

31. SHLEMIEL: SHLIMAZL::

(A) Phyllis: Mrs. Finkelstein

(B) Mrs. Finkelstein: Phyllis

(C) Me: Phyllis

(D) Phyllis: Me

32. ATONEMENT: CLEANSING::

(A) meditation: fantasy

(B) introspection: purifying

(C) OCD: sudsy

(D) clarification: sluice

GO ON TO THE NEXT PAGE

Section 1   1

S T O P

If you finish before time is called, you may correct your work using the guide below.
Do not turn to any other section in the test.

TEST ANSWERS

1. Ⓑ	9. Ⓑ	17. Ⓓ	25. Ⓐ
2. Ⓓ	10. Ⓒ	18. Ⓐ	26. Ⓐ
3. Ⓑ	11. Ⓓ	19. Ⓓ	27. Ⓓ
4. Ⓓ	12. Ⓑ	20. Ⓒ	28. Ⓓ
5. Ⓓ	13. Ⓒ	21. Ⓐ	29. Ⓒ
6. Ⓐ	14. Ⓒ	22. Ⓑ	30. Ⓒ
7. Ⓒ	15. Ⓐ	23. Ⓐ	31. Ⓑ
8. Ⓑ	16. Ⓑ	24. Ⓒ	32. Ⓑ

SIMCHAT TORAH marks the completion of (and the immediate beginning) of the reading of the Torah. Basically, once you finish the Torah, you dance a little then you open it right back up. That is IT, kids.

On Simchat Torah the scrolls are taken down from the Ark and paraded around the synagogue, and the congregation is encouraged to dance around them.

While many Jewish holidays are all about anguish, this is one holiday that is festive by design. Kids are equipped with a flag that has room at the top to secure an apple. The flags symbolize the tribal flags that the Israelites marched under. As for the apple? Well, what Jewish holiday *doesn't* have symbolism attached to harvest?

two
Simchat Torah

The one where you run around the synagogue with flags & apples.

Chai lights ®

FOR KOSHER KIDS
of All Ages

October
1976

INCLUDING **Childish** *Activities*

Hello!

Doofus and Moishey

Doofus takes Mindy's apple because she won't give him any "play."

Moishey lays the groundwork to score some "honey" by helping Mindy with her flag.

Doofus and Moishey

When it's time to dance, Doofus body-checks Moishey until he's black and blue.

Moishey shakes his groove thing proudly in honor of Simchat Torah.

Doofus and Moishey

Doofus tries to stab Moishey with his Simchat Torah flag.

Moishey delivers a scolding sermon about hurting other people.

Doofus and Moishey

Doofus disses the Torah by wiping his dirty hands on it.

Moishey respects the Torah by kissing it with feeling.

Doofus and Moishey

Doofus has fun on Simchat Torah (by stuffing his face with apples).

Moishey has fun on Simchat Torah (by doing a flag twirling routine).

THE STORY OF SHAVUOT is the tale of a woman with chutzpah named Ruth who was born a princess in a cockamamie land called Moab. When Jewish foreigners moved to her land, Ruth became smitten with a haimish mensch named Machlon and shortly thereafter became his kalleh (bride). Ruth was born a shiksa, but now practiced Judaism with real gusto. After a stroke of bad luck took the lives of her beloved husband, his brother, and his father (oy gevalt!), Ruth's mother-in-law Naomi thought "feh" and wanted to leave Moab. Naomi didn't care for Ruth to come to her Jewish homeland, but Ruth insisted that she too was a Jew, and told her "don't put the kibosh on me, you nudnik." Finally, Naomi gave Ruth a kine-ahora and relented after much kvetching. In the new homeland, Ruth worked her tuchis off to support the two of them so they didn't have to become shnorrers. She earned a farstinkener living by picking up shreds of barley in the field of a k'nocker named Boaz. And on one fateful night at Naomi's prodding, Ruth put on her best schmatte and cut a deal with Boaz to get their rightful land back. In those times women could not redeem land for themselves (sometimes a shtup was needed). Boaz kvelled and after a quickie mikvah, they married. Soon Ruth and Boaz had a little bubeleh named Ovid (who in turn had a pisher named Yishai, who was the father of King David, the redeemer of all of Israel). And after much tummel, they all lived happily every after.

three

Shavuot

The one about that lady named Ruth.

Meet Ruth!

Princess, pauper, shiksa, savior. Our girl Ruth is everything and more. Bosomy, kind, smart, loving, hardworking, a real menschette—and bosomy. Ruth not only looks great in clothes, she also looks fabulous in her knickers. Take her to a club in New York "as is" or put on one of these three outfits and imagine your own scene.

Tempting Temptress

What to wear to a shtupping? How about "almost nothing"? Panties, bra, a smile (and perhaps a blindfold). Put this outfit on Ruth for her big seduction scene with that kuni lemel, Boaz. Cut out your own cape for her "walk of shame" home early the next morning. Gevalt!

Field Gleaner Shmatte

Ruth manages to look absolutely to die for in these working-girl-slash-keeping-it-real office duds. Sure, she may be on her hands and knees all day (and night—see Tempting Temptress outfit!), but at least she looks like a million sheckles while picking up crumbs to bring home to her far-tootsed mother-in-law.

Moabite Princess

Sumptuous fur, the finest silk, and a crown made for a real princess: this outfit reminds Ruth of what she used to be in her old country—before she came to the new homeland and was forced to wear silk stockings in the humid night.

I was the kid who got a rash from just looking at anything natural. I sneezed in response to animals, large and small. At times I had so many hives that I'd name them. These unfortunate proclivities didn't make it too easy when the harvest holiday Sukkot rolled around four days after Yom Kippur. Who am I? I'm the girl who never got to live in a Sukkah, the temporary dwellings that commemorate the forty-year period during which the children of Israel wandered the desert. It's a sad story and one that could have been prevented if we only had one of these catalogs.

four

Sukkot

The one where you live in a harvest hut
and eat way too much fruit.

Vol. 5, 1951

Plotzco
SPECIALTIES

SAY GOODBYE TO BORING SUKKAHS!

The Most Trusted Name in Pre-Fab and Do-It-Yourself Sukkahs!

The "Hip-o"-Allergenic™

PL385 Comes with beaded plastic fruit, laminated wood paneling, Astroturf™ flooring, and a portal that goes directly into your house so that air conditioning can bring sweet, filtered relief. Synthetic sukkah succulence for the allergic child! (Cherry-flavored anti-histamine cream sold separately.)

™

The Mother-in-Law™

PL386   Is a bitter relative cramping your sukkah get-down? Why not try the sukkah within a sukkah? Comes with a separate area for You Know Who, featuring a convenient side entrance, special sticky tape to divide the sukkah equally, and a giant jar of aspirin.

The Inflatable™

PL387   So you live in a small apartment in the big lonely city and don't have a yard in which to entertain company? Well, move on out to the fire escape and bring a trusty friend: your blow-up Sukkah! Easy to clean, easy to store, easy to sukkah!

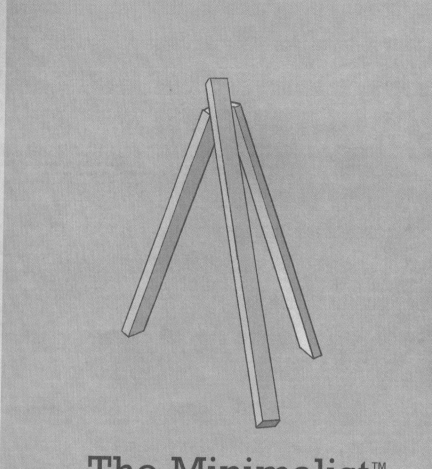

The Minimalist™

PL388   Three. Pieces. Of. Lumber.

The Organic™

The Kute Kiddie™

PL390   Washable walls, foodstuffs cut into little pieces, fluffy kid-friendly lulav, and a slip 'n' slide entryway make this sukkah kid-sational!

The Second Hand™

PL391   It was a Popsicle stick! It was a cardboard box! It was a bunch of old soda cans! Now, it's your cozy, earth-friendly sukkah! For the environmentalists out there we proudly offer sukkahs made entirely from recycled (yet not necessarily sanitary) items.

The Schmancy™

PL392 When only the finest pine, the plushest carpeting, and gourmet fruit will do, enter the most deluxe sukkah of them all. Red velvet rope included for keeping out the neighborhood riffraff. Extra large sukkah can also double as little Rifka's wedding tent, should the day ever come.

Also Available!

PL362   Sukkot wouldn't be complete without "The Four Species," which are: a citrus fruit native to Israel (or its Hebrew name, etrog), a palm branch (or lulav), two willow branches (arava), and three myrtle branches (hadas). The six branches are tied together and collectively called the lulav (the etrog is held independently). With the lulav in hand, you recite a blessing and shake the species in all six directions (east, south, west, north, up and down, symbolizing the fact that G-d is everywhere). Fun and festive! Sukkah-tastic! Free with purchase!

Just in! Kid-friendly etrogs (resistant to teeth marks!), extra large etrogs for the manly man, scented and non-scented lulavs!

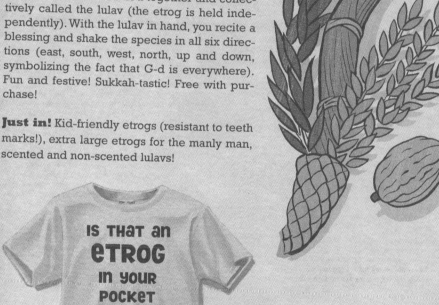

IS THAT an
eTROG
In YOUR
POCKET
OR aRe YOU
JUST HaPPY
TO see me?

PL340   Sukkot t-shirts with a variety of wonderful Sukkot messages! Check order form for favorites, or invent your own!

DECEMBER is filled with many different Christmas-themed television shows—and maybe one Hanukkah special (with nary an elf who wants to become a dentist in sight). Where is the miniseries on the Hanukkah wars starring scantily clad men? Where is the animated special where troublesome teens burn down the town while lighting a menorah? Where is the *Twilight Zone* episode where the whole world wakes up Jewish?

They say that the miracle of Hanukkah is that the oil burned in the menorah for eight nights instead of lasting only one. The real miracle is how Jews get through Christmas without going out of their minds because television on that day (actually, that whole month) is chock full of gaggy specials. Sure, the old movies are great—the first hundred times you see them. But after that, it might be more fun to actually eat the wrapping on those chocolate coins that kids get as a Hanukkah treat.

What would happen if Jews really did own the media? Would the television page feature an *I Love Lucy* marathon where the girls turn out to be wayward Jewesses? Would cartoon characters speak bad Yiddish? Would talk show hosts cook brisket for the masses?

We can only hope.

five

Hanukkah

THE ONE
WITH THE
MENORAH
AND GREASY
PANCAKES.

DECEMBER 25, 1978

MORNING

5:30 **⑤ Sermonette**
Farklempt moments to start your day, with host Shecky Farbleman and the Farble-Tone Singers.

6:00 **⑥ Goofus and Moishey—Animated in Gag-O-Vision** The boys preach their moralistic views to millions of impressionable children. On today's program Goofus lights Moishey's pupik on fire with Hanukkah candles.

⑫ It's a Wonderful Life—Movie
Jimmy Stewart and company lay on the syrup good and thick in this Frank Capra story that could never happen in real life because people are too lousy and rotten.

6:30 **⑤ G-D's Peeps**
Life affirmations for those who don't celebrate Christmas. Today: Szechuan or Cantonese?

⑥ Kimba—Smartoon Cartoon
Kimba teaches monkeys how to say Kaddish, and holds a minyan with a bunch of frogs.

7:00 **⑤ Good Morning Christian America**
Inside look at Santa Claus's controversial new memoir, "Red Suit Diaries."

⑨ Good Morning Jewish America
Today's topic: Getting through the day without smoking 400 cigarettes and drinking a quart of vodka while watching the 445th showing of "It's A Wonderful Life."

7:30 **⑥ Tuchis Patrol—Animated**
Little Fanny makes a mess of the whole mispuchah, goes meshugge on a nudnik, and then lands on her tuchis in this colorful Yiddish romp.

⑨ Kipper The Kangaroo—Live Action Smell-O-Vision Kipper and friend Whitefish get trashed on Manishchewitz with Santa's elves in the convenience store parking lot.

8:00 **⑥ Davey and Goliath—Religion**
"Yuletide Envy." Davey gets fachadded when his little Jewish friend comes over and wants to decorate his tree with matzo balls and stale Passover candy.

⑦ I Love Lucy—Marathon
Lucy accidentally slices off Ethel's finger while working at the challah factory.

⑫ It's a Wonderful Life—Movie
Do-gooder Jimmy Stewart lives in a town without one stinkin' Jew.

8:30 **⑥ Sesame Street—Children**
Elmo explains that he isn't tickled about the lack of Hanukkah shows on TV and pelts everybody with dreidels in frustration.

⑦ I Love Lucy—Marathon
Ricky goes berserk when Lucy makes an appointment for him to get circumcised.

9:00 **⑦ I Love Lucy—Marathon**
The girls get the what-for from their husbands when they spend too much gelt on fancy shmattes.

⑨ The Price Is Wholesale—Gameshow
Savvy shoppers throw baked goods at the gentile Emcee until he gives them the wholesale price of his wares.

⑪ Hanukkah Food Parade—Cooking COLOR Dancing latkes and pirouetting

Thursday
Morning

potato pancakes tell the story of Hanukkah in this schmaltzy rendition.

9:30 **7** **I Love Lucy—Marathon**
Fred gets curious about "shiksas" and when Ethel finds out she ties him up with tefillin for three days.

11 **Knish 'N' Kvetch Korner**
Eating, talking, kvetching, laughing, crying, divorcing, suing.

10:00 **7** **I Love Lucy—Marathon**
Little Rickie demands a catered briss.

12 **It's a Wonderful Life—Movie**
The four trillionth showing of the movie that you used to love.

10:30 **7** **I Love Lucy—Marathon**
Lucy plays matchmaker for lonely Mrs. Trimble by setting her up with Carlton the doorman.

13 **The Twilight Zone**

Episode: "December 25." People around the world wake up to find that all their favorite stores are closed, and there is nothing decent on TV.

11:00 **7** **I Love Lucy—Marathon**
Lucy and Ricky attend the flea market at Temple Emmanuel and get thrown out for "Jewing people down."

14 **MOVIE: Drama**
"Gidget Goes Goy!" After the little Jewess marries Moondoggie, she finds that her parents have already sat shiva for her.

11:30 **7** **I Love Lucy—Marathon**
Lucy dresses up as gefilte fish and tries to crash Ricky's Passover tribute at the club.

11 **Calvalcade of Matzo**
Your host Sheila Shleppadick cooks and sews with matzo products.

---

close up

DAIRY AND MEAT ARE FRIENDS— CARTOON
12:00 **6**

SOME THINGS JUST AREN'T MEANT TO BE
Colorful luncheon meats and wholesome Vitamin D milk teach boys and girls all over the world to be less intolerant of lactose and more kosher meat-friendly. Today Mr. Pastrami gently tells Bosco milk that he can't sit at the lunch table with him because they "don't mix."

DECEMBER 25, 1978

AFTERNOON

12:00 **6** **Dairy and Meat Are Friends—Cartoon**
Milk and meat join together to fight non-parve baked goods.

7 **I Love Lucy—Marathon**
The girls visit a slaughterhouse so they can learn how to kill meat the kosher way.

9 **Shiksathon**
Shocking activities like spreading mayonnaise on corned beef, eating pig products, and paying retail are shown in glorious, living color.

12 **It's a Wonderful Life—Movie**
Clarence the angel says to hell with getting his wings and lets Jimmy Stewart jump off the bridge.

1:00 **7** **I Love Lucy—Marathon**
Lucy performs the Heimlich maneuver on Fred during the Passover seder because of a particularly pesky piece of bitter herbs.

9 **The Gentle Gentile**
Non-Jews calmly explain why Jesus wants them to go into debt at Christmas time.

13 **Kosher Sea Salt Presents—Drama**
"It Needs More Flavor." Chaim the Salty Codfish has flavorful adventures.

1:30 **6** **Goofus and Moishey—Animated**
In Gag-O-Vision Goofus talks Moishey into getting a tattoo and then makes him cry when he tells him that now he can never, ever be buried in a Jewish cemetery.

7 **I Love Lucy—Marathon**
Fred confesses that his mother was Jewish and so now he wants to be Bar Mitzvahed at Ricky's club, the Copacabana.

11 **What's That Stink?—Gameshow**
"Cabbage, kreplach, or gefilte fish?"

2:00 **7** **I Love Lucy—Marathon**
Lucy and Ethel go orthodox and shop for new, exciting "Cher" wigs.

11 **Why Come?—Educational**
People talk in half-sentences, bungled Yiddish, and then ask "Why Come?" when they don't understand something.

12 **It's a Wonderful Life—Movie**
The townspeople confess to Jimmy Stewart that the money they collected for him is really for a new synagogue and not his farchardat savings and loan business.

2:30 **6** **Teeny Weeny Sheeny—Cartoon**
The Christian kids at school try to dip Sheeny in the baptism pool, but when they do it steams up.

7 **I Love Lucy—Marathon**
Lucy and Ethel pour bubble bath in the mikvah and cause a soapy ruckus.

9 **Team Yenta**
Your mother and her friends complain animatedly about not having any grandchildren yet.

3:00 **7** **I Love Lucy—Marathon**
Lucy sets the apartment building on fire when she tips over the Shabbat candles.

9 **General Hospital**
The townswomen feign illness to meet that hunky Dr. Kishka.

11 **READY! SET! BRISS!—Instructional**

3:30 **7** **I Love Lucy—Marathon**
Lucy and Ethel start a mail-order brisket service but have to fold when they cause an epidemic of mad cow disease.

11 **Gilligan's Island—Sitcom**
The Skipper builds sukkahs for everyone on the island. Ginger demands a bigger lulav while MaryAnn shares her cornucopia with the Professor.

13 **Rhoda—Sitcom**
Rhoda Morgenstern kicks Mary Richards's honky ass all over town after Mary kvetches

Thursday

Afternoon

about her terrible Secret Santa gift from Mr. Grant.

4:00 **7** **I Love Lucy—Marathon**
Lucy and Ethel bake X-rated hamantaschen.
12 **It's a Wonderful Life—Movie**
Jimmy Stewart converts to Judaism, leaves his hellhole of a town, and moves to New York City to work on jeweler's row.

4:30 **7** **I Love Lucy—Marathon**
Little Ricky finds the hidden matzo in Uncle Fred's pants.
11 **Name That Slur!**
"Shylock."

5:00 **7** **I Love Lucy—Marathon**
Lucy misuses her Yiddish and ends up alienating the Sisterhood when she calls Pessie Kishka "schmutzy" instead of "schmaltzy."
11 **Ku Klux Kringle—Drama**
White supremacist Santa gets into all kinds of unkosher trouble after he burns a live reindeer on someone's lawn.

5:30 **7** **I Love Lucy—Marathon**
Little Rickie plays the Lamb Shank in the story of Passover at the Hebrew School play.
9 **Family Affair—Drama**
"Oy, My Papa." Buffy and Jodi discover that their birth parents were Jewish and hold Mr. French hostage until he agrees to paint a Jewish Star in blood over their bedroom door.

EVENING

6:00 **7** **I Love Lucy—Marathon**
Lucy joins Gamblers Anonymous after playing too much dreidel.
9 **Bubbehlehs, Inc.—Crime Drama**
Feisty grandmas fight crime at the home.
12 **It's a Wonderful Life—Movie**
Hanukkah heroine Judith the Warrior arrives and cuts off mean old Mr. Potter's head.

6:30 **7** **I Love Lucy—Marathon**
Ethel feels dirty after eating a double bacon cheeseburger.
13 **This Is Your Pathetic Life, You Farstinkiner Loser**
Guests are shown embarrassing Bar Mitzvah pictures and then humiliated in front of a live audience.

7:00 **7** **I Love Lucy—Marathon**
Ricky and Fred discuss the joys of unbridled Jewish women.
11 **Jew York City**
Non-Jews try farfel for the first time and exclaim "feh."
13 **Shtupping for Dollars—Gameshow**
Contestants jew people down to win prizes.

7:30 **7** **I Love Lucy—Marathon**
Lucy orders pork chops at the local steakhouse and is banished from the kingdom of the Upper West Side forever.
9 **Pick a Plague—Game show**
Tonight's challenge: Dodging locusts!

8:00 **7** **I Love Lucy—Marathon**
The girls have a fight when Ethel insists Lucy sacrifice Little Ricky for Passover.

DECEMBER 25, 1978

11 **Movie—Musical**
"Huckleberry Finnberg." A tuneful adaptation of the classic tale of a Yeshiva student and his adventures on the Mississippi. (Filmed on location in Brooklyn).

12 **It's a Wonderful Life—Movie**
In this cartoon version, fruits and vegetables play all characters.

8:30 **5** **What's Happening?!**
Rerun joins a dance contest and does the hora until he drops. Shirley starts serving kosher salami at the diner.

7 SPECIAL **Man Oh Manischewitz!—Mystery** Jews on Christmas search for the one open movie theatre before they tear all the hair out of their collective heads.

9:00 **9** **Little House on the Pogrom—Drama**
The Ingallstein family kills Jesus in this touching family teleplay.

11 **Hanukkah Horse Race**
Gamblers Anonymous presents interactive betting. Outstanding eligibles: Li'l Pisher, Knedlach 'n' Liver, Mogen David.

9:30 **9** **True Hollywood Story—"Dentist Elf"**
For the first time on TV, Hermie tells us of his desperation to leave Santa's digs because of inappropriate touching in the workshop. (May not be suitable for children.)

13 **Celebrity Mohel—Gameshow**
Fun with babies and knives.

10:00 **7** **The Shlemiel World**
"Sometimes I Feel Like a Bagel-less Child."

Sheltered Jewish twentysomethings are dropped into America's heartland and left to fend for themselves without a Loehmann's or Jewish deli nearby.

12 **It's a Wonderful Life—Movie**
Jimmy Stewart sports payess and tall black hats after he is reborn as an Orthodox rebbe.

10:30 **7** **Singalong—Teenage**
Singer-songwriters play your favorite Passover tunes. Highlight: "Chad Gadya"—acoustic.

9 **COPS**
"Hymietown, This Ain't." A yellow school bus filled with Chassids is pulled over by a back-woods cop.

11:00 **11** **Steinfeld**
The Jewish version of the hit show "Seinfeld."

25 **Schvitz-Tastic—Paid Programming**

11:30 **9** **Perry Masonfeld—Mystery**
"The Case of the Onge Potcheked."

11 **Friends—Comedy**
The gang tries to figure out why Ross and Monica don't celebrate Rosh Hashanah even though a big Jew plays their father on the show.

11:30 **42** **The Twilight Zone**
Episode: "If Jews Ruled The World." People of earth crave overcooked vegetables at precisely the same time.

12:00 **12** **It's a Wonderful Life**
Christmas is finally over and indeed, it is a wonderful life.

FLASHBACK: It's the month of March, in the late 1970s. There is a girl in a yellow flower-powered bedroom watching television and listening to records at the same time while her older sister is trying on a Queen Esther outfit for the Purim parade at the synagogue. The sister is squealing at the sight of her mother's handiwork, as there are lots of hand-sewn sequins on this satiny cloth and a matching crown made from extra thick tin foil. The girl is concentrating on the TV while singing lyrics to the old-school rap record. She notices that her Queen Vashti outfit is really a Halloween costume from the drugstore. However that doesn't bother her for she is dreaming—dreaming of a Purim movie starring her favorite sitcom actors. She envisions a big budget extravaganza complete with a rap soundtrack to add spice. How fantastic, she thinks, Purim has it all: juicy roles for women, fun-to-watch bad guys, ethnic pride, and even a beheading.

Her mother calls her and tells her it's time to attend the Purim bazaar, but the girl tells her mother that she is sick and needs to stay home. As soon as her parents leave she puts on her Queen Vashti outfit for inspiration. The girl reaches for her favorite pen (the one with four different color inks) and her charcoals. She starts to write her version of the Purim story and to sketch out scene studies. She does this for many hours, still in her Queen Vashti outfit. And in the blue glow of the television set the girl finishes her masterpiece.

WORD 'EM UP, IT'S A PURIM THING Y'ALL.

six

Purim

The one they call
Jewish Halloween.

Word 'Em Up — It's A Purim Thang, Y'all

<u>Cast:</u>
King AHASVERUS — King of Persia
Queen VASHTI — The King's first wife
HAMAN — The King's right-hand man
Queen ESTHER — The King's second wife
MORDECHAI — ESTHER's cousin

SCENE 1

INTERIOR: KING AHASVERUS'S ROYAL CRIB.
The King is cold kickin' it with his boyz and some big bottles
of grape wine and knish pockets snack treats. His Queen, VASHTI,
is by his side looking bored and twirling her corn-rowed hair.

VASHTI
I'm not feeling groovy.

AHASVERUS
(feeling disrespected)
Boo, I want you buck nekkid and on display for my peeps! (He
snaps his fingers into a "z")

VASHTI
Puh-lease (she wrings her neck). I'm going to get a nice baloney
sandwich instead.

AHASVERUS is surrounded by his homies, namely sitcom extras from
back in the day, including the sweathogs from Brooklyn. VASHTI
recoils openly as AHASVERUS tries to make her dance.

AHASVERUS
(In a threatening voice)
Girl, I KNOW you don't want me to get Haman on your booty.

At the mention of HAMAN's name, VASHTI starts buggin'. HAMAN is
the King's henchman, the man with the juice, not to mention a

penchant for cutting people's heads off. VASHTI makes a flourish
with her hand and starts to leave the room but is grabbed by
HAMAN, who is waiting in the wings. The sound of a sword is
heard and then a thud. Enter HAMAN, who "soul city" walks into
the room.

HAMAN

Bro, Vashti was all up in your grill up to the minute before I
had her whacked.

AHASVERUS

I know you had to ice her, dog. Business — never personal. Vashti
was aiiight and all, but I need me an around-the-way girl. No
more Valley girls who front.

HAMAN

Casket closed. So why don't you get yourself another queen? And
not one with a weave! You feelin' me?

AHASVERUS

I'm the King, not a pimp!

HAMAN

Leave it to me. I'll get in the jeep, go beep, and your house
will be full of honeys. Aiiight?

AHASVERUS

(Fluffing his Afro)

Aiiight. Set it off for tonight.

SCENE 2

INTERIOR: KING AHASVERUS'S ROYAL CRIB.
Later that same night, AHASVERUS's royal crib has been turned
into what looks like a strip club. Wine is flowing and there are
many lovely ladies in attendance, including some girls flown in
from a little house near a prairie, and some girls from a board-
ing school in Peekskill, New York.

                              AHASVERUS
                              (to HAMAN)
        Damn! These are the finest females in all of Persia, especially
                that lovely lady over there with the big Afro.

HAMAN cuts through the crowd to procure this female for the KING.
Her name is ESTHER and she is with her cousin and chaperone for
the evening, MORDECHAI.

                              HAMAN
        The King would like to check out your fine self.

                              ESTHER
                           (not impressed)
                 Are you talkin' to me, shortstuff?

                              HAMAN
        (Taken aback at her brazenness, he turns to MORDECHAI)
                 This is ladies night, bro. Step.

59

MORDECHAI

Oh, but that is *the* reason to be here. Why, I see some ladies
right now that might like to make a Mordechai sammich.
Oh, Ladies . . .

HAMAN puts his hand in MORDECHAI's face and mushes him. Then he
takes ESTHER by the arm and shunts her to the KING.

AHASVERUS
(flashes a big smile to show his gold teeth)
What is your name, sweet thing?

ESTHER
(still not impressed)
Esther, but you can call me *Miss* Esther. Stop jockin' me before I
start clockin' you. When are you gonna play some Kool and the
Gang?

AHASVERUS
Ah, you like the old school. You ready to get-up with the get-
down?

ESTHER
Just as long as I'm not let-down. What is up with all these baby-
oiled females on strip poles? I do not (wringing her neck) think
that's cute. I'm about to jet on up outta here.

AHASVERUS
Hey, baby girl, don't sweat it, *let* it.

ESTHER
Let me break it down for you, okaaay? (finger snap) What if one of
these women was your sister? Or your mother?

AHASVERUS
(astounded yet turned on by the woman)
Nobody ever broke it down for me like that. I feel that.

ESTHER
Damn skippy. Now, King, let's get this party started right!

ESTHER and the KING boogie for hours. They are still dancing well
into the next morning and are both feeling the love connection.

AHASVERUS
(during a slow jam)
Where you been all my life? How could such a fly honey live so
close by and yet I've never stepped to you?

ESTHER
I'm in the 'hood, mostly, taking care of my business.

AHASVERUS
Well, I'd like to take care of your business too. But what is up
with your cousin slash chaperone?

                              ESTHER
He may look like a skinny chickenhead but he gets crazy phat props
       from me. Don't worry, 'Rosh, you're my main man.

                            FADE OUT.

                             SCENE 3

INTERIOR: KING AHASVERUS'S ROYAL CRIB
ESTHER and AHASVERUS wed shortly thereafter and things are chill.
The only time things get hectic is when MORDECHAI comes to visit.
AHASVERUS is down with him, but HAMAN doesn't dig him.

                              HAMAN
                Yo man, Esther's cousin is *ill*.
He needs to show me respect. He says that he won't bow to me, only
                  to G-d. What is up with *that*?

                            AHASVERUS
                 (tired of hearing HAMAN kvetch)
              He's a brotha, so don't sweat it . . .

                              HAMAN
                           (disgusted)
                       I know, *let* it.

                            AHASVERUS
       Enough already! Do what you got to do but leave me out of it
        tonight. Esther and I will be cold lampin' on the down low.

HAMAN knows why he doesn't like MORDECHAI. It's because he's down

with the brotherhood — the brotherhood of Jews! And since the KING won't hear the real 411 about MORDECHAI, HAMAN decides to take matters into his own hands with an army that seems to be made up from the kids of *Fame*.

                        HAMAN
         (to a bunch of dancers, piano players and assorted extras)
     You heard me! I said six feet deep. If Mordechai can't respect me,
     then I want to ice *all* of the Jews! I don't care how you do it—
     pirouette them into the ground—but I want every Jew in Persia
                        pushing up daisies.

                        SCENE 4

INTERIOR: KING AHASVERUS'S ROYAL BEDROOM
ESTHER finds out about HAMAN's wack plot and starts doing the
freak-freak down the street-street because she never told the KING
that she is Jewish. Knowing that she could flip the script on her
heritage and play dumb, she knows that she must school the King
for real.

                        ESTHER
     Your boy Haman is off the hook. You know what that fool wants to
          do? He wants to kill all the Jews in Persia!

                        AHASVERUS
             Get your bootyliciousness over here.
     Haman's got issues fo' sure but why you buggin' bugaboo?

                    ESTHER
              (not able to contain herself)
Because I'm down with the tribe, yo! I'm Jewish and so is my whole
posse! And if Haman has his way, we'll all be ov-ah. (Finger snap)
              Is that how it's gonna be? You tell me.

                    AHASVERUS
Damn, baby girl! I don't care that you're Jewish. All I know is
           that you are fiiine and you are miiine.

                    ESTHER
              (relieved but not showing it)
Cool. Now let's find Haman. I wanna put a shoe right up his . . .

                    SCENE 5

INTERIOR: CASTLE FOYER
HAMAN is in the castle foyer, trying on one of the king's crowns.
AHASVERUS and ESTHER bum-rush him.

                    HAMAN
              (startled)
I thought you two was hanging out upstairs.

                    ESTHER
I'd like to hang *you* out, you no good lowdown dirty shame.

                    HAMAN
              (in a tizzy)

King, I'm your boy. Come on, tell her that I'm your boy.

                         AHASVERUS
You ain't my boy. I heard what you were trying to throw down. I'm
gonna kick you to the curb like a redheaded stepchild.

                          ESTHER
             Haman, honey, think of it this way.
             The devil made him do it!

HAMAN is taken away and placed on a hard labor kibbutz. The king
and queen then invite MORDECHAI and all of their peeps over to
their crib. AHASVERUS and MORDECHAI even have a dance-off and when
MORDECHAI body-pops for the fourth hour straight, AHASVERUS deems
him his new jack.

                         MORDECHAI
          Bless this wine. Bless this hiz-ouse.
           Bless Esther and bless Ahasverus.
           I think y'all are . . . dy-no-mite!

                       THE END, Yo

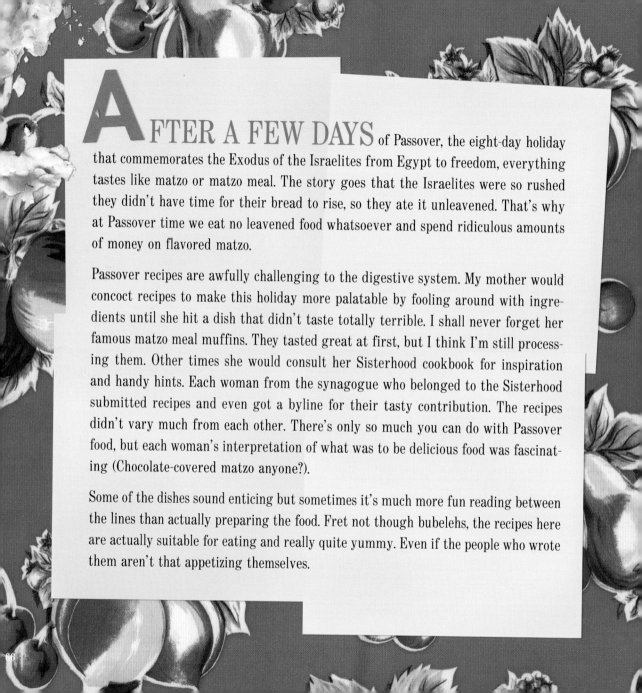

AFTER A FEW DAYS of Passover, the eight-day holiday that commemorates the Exodus of the Israelites from Egypt to freedom, everything tastes like matzo or matzo meal. The story goes that the Israelites were so rushed they didn't have time for their bread to rise, so they ate it unleavened. That's why at Passover time we eat no leavened food whatsoever and spend ridiculous amounts of money on flavored matzo.

Passover recipes are awfully challenging to the digestive system. My mother would concoct recipes to make this holiday more palatable by fooling around with ingredients until she hit a dish that didn't taste totally terrible. I shall never forget her famous matzo meal muffins. They tasted great at first, but I think I'm still processing them. Other times she would consult her Sisterhood cookbook for inspiration and handy hints. Each woman from the synagogue who belonged to the Sisterhood submitted recipes and even got a byline for their tasty contribution. The recipes didn't vary much from each other. There's only so much you can do with Passover food, but each woman's interpretation of what was to be delicious food was fascinating (Chocolate-covered matzo anyone?).

Some of the dishes sound enticing but sometimes it's much more fun reading between the lines than actually preparing the food. Fret not though bubelehs, the recipes here are actually suitable for eating and really quite yummy. Even if the people who wrote them aren't that appetizing themselves.

seven

Passover

The one with the big crackers.

THE TEMPLE BETH H'ELL
SISTERHOOD
COOKBOOK

Charoset

6 large apples, peeled and chopped
²/₃ cup walnuts
3 tablespoons sugar
1 teaspoon cinnamon
¹/₄ cup sweet red wine

Charoset is symbolic of the mortar used by Hebrew slaves to build Egyptian structures. Keep that in mind when it comes to texture. First, combine all the ingredients, even though someone who shall remain nameless (DOT ROSENCRANZ) borrowed your food processor and then never returned it. Using your hand mixer, blend everything together and try not to think about how angry you are at the vilder chaya who stole this recipe from you then claimed it as her own (FERN FESHER). Add more wine (and whine) as you go. Keep the consistency crunchy, like my meshuggener daughter and her hairy armpits. Stop when exhausted.

Pessie Kishka

Knaidlach Matzo Balls with Liver

Matzo meal
A little salt
Some sugar
6 eggs
Oil
Salt to taste
$^1/_2$ pound chicken livers
More salt
3 tablespoons chicken fat

Combine the matzo meal, salt, sugar, and eggs.
You can use a food processor, but I don't have
one, thanks to someone (PESSIE KISHKA). Add
enough matzo meal to make a tight yet loose
ball. It should remind you of that awful caftan
that someone (MIG FARFELLE) wore to her son's
wedding. Boil salted water and add the matzo
balls until they are done but not like when
someone (PESSIE KISHKA) cooks steak, burns it,
and calls it "done." The balls should be on the
hard side (PESSIE KISHKA). Add oil to a frying
pan and sauté the chicken livers with salt
until you can feel your blood pressure rise
just by smelling what's in the pan. When you
can mash the livers with a fork, drain them and
put them into a large bowl. Add the chicken fat
and shake the bowl vigorously. Pour this mixture over the matzo balls and shake again, like
someone (FERN FESHER) after one glass of Mogen
David (but you didn't hear that from me).
Transfer to a baking dish and cook in a 300-
degree oven until warm. Eat it up!

Dot Rosencranz

Fried Matzo

3 boards of matzo
1 egg
$\frac{1}{2}$ cup water or milk
Salt to taste
Sugar to taste
1 tablespoon oil OR butter OR onion-flavored fat
OR chicken fat

Break the matzo boards into pieces. It's easy.
Just imagine someone's bony tuchis (DOT ROSEN-
CRANZ), and snap, 1-2-3. Wet them in the water
or milk and then drain, reserving the liquid.
Make sure they are not soggy (like PESSIE
KISHKAH's sponge cake). In a bowl, beat the egg
like someone (MIG FARFELLE) does her farcocka-
mamie husband (but I'm not saying nothin') with
the reserved liquid, salt, sugar. Dip the matzo
pieces into the egg mixture, but do not dip
your fingers into this for a little taste (I'm
talking to you, DOT ROSENCRANZ). Heat the oil or
fat in a frying pan and cook the egg-dipped
matzo pieces until golden brown. Sprinkle with
cinnamon and sugar—or honey, if you like, but
not too much, like someone (PESSIE KISHKA) does,
because it ruins the whole thing.

Fern Fesher

Mig's Banana Fritters

3 eggs, beaten
1 teaspoon salt
³/₄ cup water
1 teaspoon cinnamon
1 ¹/₄ cups matzo meal
2 large firm bananas, sliced

Combine eggs, salt, water, sugar, and cinnamon in the food processor that you know was regifted to you from someone (PESSIE KISHKA). Mix in the matzo meal and gently add the bananas. Do not smash them, even though it is hard to restrain yourself when you conjure up someone's face (FERN FESHER) and then imagine how gratifying it would be to stick a fork in it. In someone's (DOT ROSENCRANZ'S) frying pan which you are not returning to her until she apologizes for saying you know what to you know who you know where, heat an inch of hot fat, or pinch an inch of someone (FERN FESHER), and you're good to go. Make tablespoon-size drops and fry until golden brown. Drain well on paper towels and serve with sour cream. Perfection!

Mig Farfelle

Tuna Fish Gefilte Fish

1 can white meat tuna (or if you're a cheapo like
   PESSIE KISHKA, you'd use that chunk light variety)
2 eggs lightly beaten (like your face in my dreams,
   FERN FESHER)
1 grated onion
4 teaspoons matzo meal
Salt and pepper
1 quart water (not stinkin' tap water, MIG FARFELLE)
Onions, sliced (like you need it for your breath,
   DOT ROSENCRANZ)
Sliced carrots

Empty the tuna into a bowl and hold your nose if
you use the bargain brand (PESSIE KISHKA, you shame
us all). Add the eggs, the grated onion and the
matzo meal. Sprinkle with salt and pepper. Make
balls (think of your husband, MIG FARFELLE, I sure
will!) of the mixture. Boil water in a pot (but not
in DOT ROSENCRANZ's cookware because she doesn't
wipe it well) and add the vegetables and spices.
Place (not throw like a wild beast, PESSIE KISHKA)
the tuna balls into the water. Cook over low heat
until the vegetables are soft (like FERN FESHER's
noggin), and chow down.

The Committee

PEOPLE LIE.

Sometimes it's to protect your feelings ("No, you don't look fat in that at all!"). Sometimes it's because they're embarrassed ("I did not have sex with that woman!"). And sometimes it's because they are mean ("Yes, all the quarters you collect for trees in Israel will go straight to a lovely orchard in beautiful downtown Israel-city.").

Not everyone lies. Your parents certainly never lied to you, did they? ("Thunder is merely G-d vacuuming.") And the doctors never lied to you either, did they? (This won't hurt a bit.) And your boyfriend always told you the truth, right? ("It's not you, it's me.") And when your Hebrew school-teacher tells you that he is taking all the money that you collected to plant trees in Israel, you should totally, totally trust him and believe his words because he would never lie to you, right?

OK then, I believe you.

SURE I DO.

eight

Tu Bishvat

the one where
They take your quarters to
"Plant trees in Israel."

Mr. EDitor
THE New York Times
New York, U.S.A.

Dear Editor,

I have been silent for TOO long. Now is the
time to BLOW The COVER on "Tu Bishvat."
Herewith is my gripping story. PLEASE Listen.
If necessary, take a break ~~and~~ to go ~~to~~ to the bathroom
or to get yourself a Cookie. But Please, come
right back to this letter. I'm Waiting for You!

This has been "nagging" at me ever since I
was a ~~little~~ young girl, hair in a snood,
sitting at a fake wood table in a poorly vent-
ilated room labeled "HIGHEr Jewish EDUCATION".
I always knew ~~that~~ that something was FISHY
about the Jewish holiday Tu Bishvat. Technically
the name means the fifteenth (15th) day ~~in~~ the
Jewish month of Shvat (February!), which
was historically the last day or the tax year
for assessing the fruitfulness of trees. It was
basically an inventory for trees and the fruit they
bear and to celebrate that you are ~~to~~ supposed to
eat the fruit from said trees. I know what you're
thinking: This is a celebration?!! Anyway, the ~~st~~

y = my Gullibili
x = mr. Levitt's
earning abili

)(42)

'1 ( )

)(42)

'1(x) =

(42) =

'1(x)

Today
I AM
A WoMan

SAP!!

Sap supposedly rises on that day, and to commemorate it people "get down" by — you guessed it — EATING FRUIT. Yes, another ~~holiday~~ festival involving the eating of fruit. When's the holiday about taking antacid for all the BLOATING? I'll be first in line to celebrate THAT!!

Like many other Jewish kids, I learned about this holiday in Hebrew school. My teacher, a nebbish named Mr. Levitt (name NOT changed), told us that Tu Bishvat was a celebration of trees and their fruitfulness. Trees? Fruit? Please, hadn't we eaten enough ~~trees~~ fruit during Sukkot? I had other things on my mind. Such as, when I was going to fill out my bra. (Stop looking at me like that!!).

Speaking of sap rising, look at how I leapt from my seat in Mr. Levitt's class when he told me to start collecting money to plant trees in Israel because it was Tu Bishvat. This entailed me ringing doorbells and begging for quarters. "NO, I'm sorry. I'm not a Girl Scout with cookies. I am a little Jewish girl who needs quarters for trees. Help me. The sap must rise."

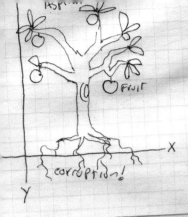

aspir...

Fruit

X

corruption!

Y

✓ Isralien

Scorpio

✓ Levitt

1 I AM THAT SAP.

Surprisingly, I got a lot of Money. It seemed that people liked planting trees in Israel. Why shouldn't they have? It's not like THEY had to do the planting themselves! It's not like THEY had to care for them and ~~free~~ LOVE them and fertilize them, then water them too much and Kill them! It was just a few quarters. After I turned in all <u>FORTY-TWO DOLLARS</u> worth ~~$42~~ of quarters to one Mr. Levitt - a man clad in navy blue corduroys and a velvet yarmulke that said "SCORPIO" on it - I didn't think much of it. Maybe I should have gotten a reciept for all those bicentennial quarters, but I wasn't that kind of kid. NAH, I turned in my gelt and started to think of my impending bat mitzvah instead.

I worked long and hard to prepare my Torah portion. I agonized over my dress. I did my own seating arrangements, placing the two cutest boys in my class on either side of me. It would all be perfect. Please try to picture it Sir or Madam who is reading this now. It was a snowy winter night. Practically a blizzard. It was terrible weather outside. Dangerous and beautiful.

slippery yet calm. I shall never forget it, for this was the night when I became a 🌼 WOMAN 🌼.
↑ Flowers! It's a motif!

In snowboots and pink barrettes, I belted out my Torah portion. I kissed all the smelly relatives who ~~all~~ stunk like dentures and mothballs. I even was nice to my younger brother. But when all was said and done and the night was over, I had to face the ugly truth about my bat mitzvah gifts. There were no charm bracelets, hip huggers, candy necklaces, or big hoop earrings awaiting me, but TREES PLANTED IN MY NAME IN ISRAEL. And it wasn't even Tu Bishvat! I wished I could do my Torah portion all over again. I'd start with a loud "BARUCH ATOY I'M ANNOYED."

Summoning my inner Helen Reddy, I said out loud to nobody in particular, "Keep it together young Jewish woman." So I've got trees. All right, then, that's something. Maybe one day I could visit ~~my~~ my trees, cut them down and make a house for myself.

THAT NEVER HAPPENED. Look at the above paragraph. Ask yourself, how does a bat mitzvah girl deal with this? Maybe I should have demanded pictures of my trees' growth. Maybe the money never went to buying trees. Tu Bishvat is hardly ~~a~~

mentioned in Jewish literature, and if you ask Jews exactly what it is, they'll look at you blankly and then say something about it being "the one about the trees."

FACT: In 1972, I gave my Hebrew-school ~~teacher~~ teacher almost $42 in quarters to purchase trees in Israel.

FACT: I knocked on doors and searched the sofa for renegade coins to put toward tree planting.

FACT: Levitt took at least six cardboard pamphlets filled with quarters, which should have been enough to garner me a small orchard somewhere in Israel.

FACT: That was the last I saw of the money.
FACT: After recieving ugly cards with the announcement "A tree was planted in Israel for you," not only did I never see any pictures of my trees, but I never even received a LEAF
FACT: I never got any updates on my saplings
FACT: I never even got dry rot.
FACT: I ask you again, who is the SAP now?
~~FACT~~

→ I KNOW SOMETHING. SOMEONE has ~~taken~~ taken my trees for HIMSELF and sold them for cash, cut them down, and made them into furniture.

I feel sick. Maybe I am sitting on my sapling right now. I could cry. I'm crying now. The TEARS STILL FLOW.

Sometimes I think that there are no trees at all and there never were. ISRAEL IS A DESERT, HOW CAN THERE BE TREES?!! Trees is a code word for something else. But what ????? Is it all a joke? Is it a way of getting out of giving real gifts, such as a gold dog tag necklace, scented soaps, or a nice little pair of toe socks? How many times have you said "I'll plant a tree in Israel for you," with a wink when you've shown up giftless to ~~the~~ someone's affair? I KNOW YOU HAVE. Schmuck.

IF MY TREES IN ISRAEL EXISTED, THEN ALL OF THOSE TOUR GROUPS WOULD HAVE PICTURES OF THEMSELVES NEXT TO THEM BECAUSE THEY ARE SO BEAUTIFUL! Where are those pictures? Where are my trees? Where are my quarters.???!

POSSIBLE SCENARIOS

A— I have a queasy sick and sad vision of Mr. Levitt sitting high on the nonkosher hog

Scorpio
Scorpio
Scorpio
Scorpio
Scorpio
Scorpio
Scorpio
Scorpio

in great ~~sug~~ luxury somewhere with one of the ladies from ~~the~~ the Sisterhood from the money I collected for the trees. Perhaps in a tree house made from my DEAD TREES. I hate him!!!
Plausibility: 6.5
Possibility: 4.5

B- It was the ISRaliens! (A group vastly underreported in your newspaper I might add.) These half Israeli - half - aliens have landed in Israel and are using the trees for menacing Purposes. They are probably eating the trees and/or using their transparent spaceships to transport the ~~trees~~ trees and their unwilling ~~saplings~~ saplings to their home planet.
Plausibility: 9
Possibility: 10 !!!

PLEASE, Please, help me find the trees. The Israeliens, Mr. Levitt and all the LIARS out there aren't allowed to have them. They're MINE. AND YOURS!!!!!

Love,

(Please don't print my name. I don't want the Israeliens to find me! Also, my mother would be very Upset.)

Where does it END?!!

$S' = Scorpio$
$S^2 = SAP$

$S^2 (.25)(4)($

$S^2 ($42$)$

$S'(\text{ })$

$\dfrac{S^2}{S'(0}$

$\dfrac{S^2 (412)}{S'(\text{Tu Bishvat})}$

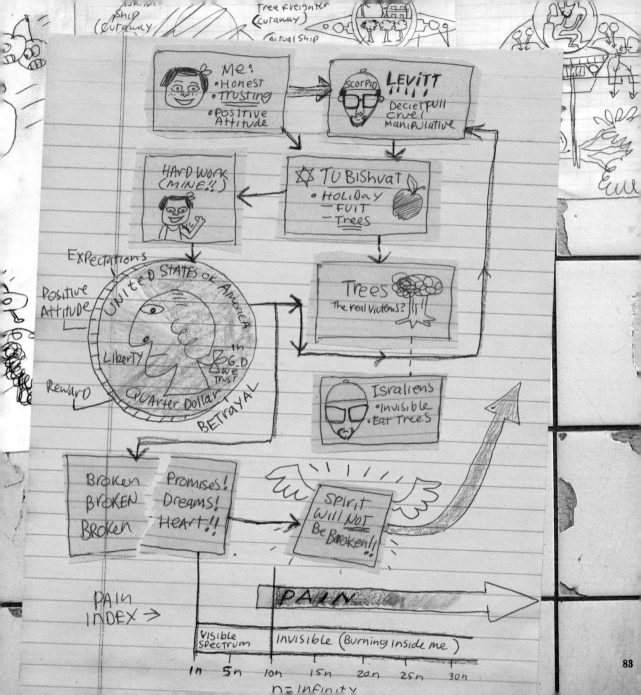

83

SHABBAT

SHABBAT is about doing nothing. It is the time of the week to reflect deeply, sometimes without using electricity or driving a car. It's not about going out with your girlfriends to get smashed on $10 martinis or working late at the office or having an awkward date with some guy who lied about everything in his personal ad. And even though some synagogues now host a "Meat and Greet" for Jewish singles, it really isn't about that either (unless he's a successful doctor!).

If you're Jewish, on Friday nights you are supposed to drag yourself to the synagogue to partake in the joy of Shabbat. This usually includes singing songs, praying, and scoping the congregation to see who got engaged that week. This all can prove to be entertaining as well as enlightening except for the fact that it takes you away from really good Friday-night TV.

Doing nothing sounds easy enough but when you're a kid, it can be a real drag, especially when every other kid in the neighborhood is riding their bikes and popping excellent wheelies in front of your bedroom window. It's not much easier when you get older either. Particularly when that one nice Jewish guy finally asks you out on a date. So, is it naughty to go out on Shabbat? Certainly not! That is, as long as you "do nothing."

nine

Shabbat

The one where you can't do stuff because it's Saturday.

C✡NNECTI✡NS

WOMEN SEEKING NON-JEWISH MEN

TOGETHA FOREVA WHATEVA
Woman seeking man for marriage. Can be Jewish, black, Asian, purple, I don't care anymore. I am a lively 40ish gal looking to settle down with a nice fella. I have: money, brains, and a kosher kitchen. You have: job, house, and teeth.

LEGGY LANSKY
Young Barbra Streisand type ("Funny Girl" era) looking for dark, handsome non-Jewish man who will make her mother sit shiva for her because he's not Jewish. Let's drive everybody crazy!

FORESKIN FRIENDLY
Daring lady seeks manly men for frolic-some fun. Cutters not welcome. Looking for natural men. I'll show you mine if you show me yours!

JEWISH WOMEN SEEKING JEWISH MEN

I AM ALL THAT. ARE YOU?
Undemanding Jewish woman seeks man who is at least 6'tall, handsome as sin, has thick hair, no facial growth, house in Hamptons, boat, season tickets to the Met, synagogue seats for the High Holy Days, Upper West Side condo, who likes to cook, do laundry, and clean. Be very, very wealthy. Please send photo and bank statement.

THE WHOLE MISCHPUCAH
Sweet, petite, nice feet—that's me! I'm succulent like Sukkot fruit, can rise to the occasion like challah bread and enjoy sleep-ing with a sheet between us during "those times of the month."

HIGH CHOLESTEROL
Fertility-ready lady aching to quiet mother's incessant yammering about having no grandchildren is looking for sperm-active man. Let's meet and marry today and fulfill grandchild quotient. I'm ovulating NOW!

MUCH ADO ABOUT SCHTUPPING
Frisky Jewish lady searching for SWJM. Let's meet and not necessarily go out to dinner, movies, museums, parks, picnics, baseball games, or anywhere in public.

MEN SEEKING JEWISH WOMEN

MAMA'S BOY NEEDS TO BE SPANKED
You are gorgeous, sexy, Jewish and like to cook and clean up after me. I am: devilish, cuddly, chubby, and will "do everything."

MODERN-DAY AHASVERUS IS LOOKING FOR HIS QUEEN ESTHER.
Let's spend Purim together "making hamantaschen." Prune flavor?

LINEAR KVETCHING
Erudite Jewish scholar seeks female with Ph.D to solve dilemmas such as kosherness in the modern world, payess as fashion statements, and to complain bitterly about the new tune for Hebrew songs like "Adom Olam." Good punctuation a plus.

LOOKING FOR MRS. JEWISH RIGHT
You like to wear headscarves, get pregnant, and prepare elaborate Sabbath dinners. Let's meet for segregated praying!

KISS ME, I'M JEWISH
SWJM into Bette Midler, not mixing dairy with meat, cursing in Yiddish loudly—and YOU, if you're glatt kosher and like to wear wigs!

ARE YOU MY MOMMY?
Looking for woman 60-85 for Jewish mothering. Wants desperately to regress. Toilet trained.

IS THE RUMOR TRUE?
Sexy guy into hot sex is looking for one of those unbridled Jewish dames. Not a joke. First drink on me.

JEWISH MEN SEEKING NON-JEWISH WOMEN

OF MICE AND MENSCH
Romantic Jewish guy looking for shiksational woman to lavish with love and matzo. Let me feed you kreplach and chicken soup! Must be a natural blonde and willing to put up with annual Passover seder.

SOME LIKE IT GOYISHE!
Hot SWJM (Jewish by birth but looks Italian) looking for hot SWF. Let's eat mayonnaise on corned beef recklessly!

DENTED KNIGHT
Knight in slightly dented armor seeking non-Jewish American princess who won't break my balls.

MOTHER'S GONE, NOW I CAN BE HAPPY
Me: Rich Jewish man who is healthy, fit, and just inherited a huge apartment on the Upper East Side. You: Protestant Goddess who secretly longs for Jewish man who will ultimately ruin things by suffocating her and being too self-deprecating.

JEWISH WOMEN SEEKING JEWISH WOMEN

TENDER IS THE SCHMALTZ
I have a knish and you have the mustard. Let's make a meal together. Extra apple-sauce is yours if you speak Hebrew fluently.

RED BADGE OF CHUTZPAH
Synagogue librarian is seeking Jewish literary-minded women to know better. form a sisterhood!

WOMEN'S MIKVAH GROUP
Fleshy women encouraged to let loose cleanse together in a spiritual setting

JEWISH MEN SEEKING JEWISH ME

DON'T TELL BUBBEY!
SWJM seeks same. Let's meet discret and enjoy ourselves the way the guys di the uncut version of *Spartacus*.

CIRCUMCISION A MUST
Looking for a nice Jewish guy who likes party hard and pray hard. Let's shlep around together, sometimes quoting To then go out for hot fun.

FAYGELAS NEED NOT APPLY
Ungay gay Jewish man looking for ungay Jewish man. Also, I'm looking for someo who doesn't normally respond to perso ads. Please write!

IS THIS YOU?

You: sensational woman browsing gefi fish aisle wearing Bon Jovi t-shirt. I wa opposite you in a brown leisure suit. Intestinal gas prohibited me from speak

We were waiting for the M9 bus and sp of schmutz. I'd like to see you again a talk more about our common interest

Brooklyn supermarket shopper: you: ra bow fanny-pack, sunglasses, clodhoppe Me: rubber thongs, relaxed fit jeans, wo weary look. We passed each other longi in frozen foods. "Peas" call me.

Oy Vey Moment: met on the crowded Q t last February during "sick passenger." in winter seersucker, me in purple felt co Still regret not passing you my number. be in the same car from now on. Find m

SECTS AND THE CITY
by GOLDIE LOX

Shabbat Shalom
Week One

I've wanted to reconnect with my Jewish roots (not the brown ones; I still plan to be a blonde) so I accepted a date with a nice Orthodox young man named Mr. Jig. Jig wore pressed black suits, proper hats, and shiny black shoes. I was so mesmerized by his appearance that I found myself saying "yes" when Jig asked me to go to his shul with him on Friday night. I hadn't had time to think this whole date through and had so much to ponder. Like, what kind of shoes do I wear to Shabbat services anyway?

Since Jig was Orthodox he couldn't drive until sunset the next day and so I arrived at his apartment courtesy of a twelve-dollar taxicab. Our meeting place was a tenement building on the Lower East Side that doubled as gallery space during the week. Jig was talking to an old couple with white hair and dramatic black clothing. Sort of a Helmut Lang-meets-Orchard Street type of thing. I strolled over to Mr. Jig in my demure kitten-heels. How good did I look?

"You want for me to get you a shawl," the woman said, registering no modulation in her voice.

Before I had a chance to decline this bizarre offer, this woman that turned out to be Jig's mother tossed a wrap the size of a small blanket over me. This was weird. Only a shmendrick would bring his parents on a date. The senior Mr. Jig grunted in my direction and his mother sounded like a tape loop of *tsk tsk* sounds. I felt as if I was the shiksa at the mikvah and had to wonder: Was I?

Jig led me into the beautifully decrepit synagogue. Just as I was imagining us getting married in here, we stopped in front of a stairway. I contemplated how to maneuver my Manolos up the steps as Jig disappeared behind a curtain. Maybe this is foreplay, I thought. That is, until Mama Jig guided me up the stairs to the women's section. Downstairs, the men sang the prayers joyously and even danced around with each other. Upstairs I sat amidst a group of females firmly planted in their seats who didn't find anything even slightly offensive about being cordoned off from the men. I had to ask myself, should I go down and start a conga line?

It was nice to hear Hebrew, even if I had no idea what was being said. I reminisced (in inflective voiceover to myself) about Jewish things like my Bat Mitzvah and the first time I slept with a Jewish boy. Forty-five minutes later Mrs. Jig nudged me with her elbow and I came to. We went outside where I stood on the street corner and primped until Jig slowly ambled over to me. The way he didn't react to my hair twirling and frequent cleavage squeezes was confusing. That's when Jig calmly told me that our time together was over. According to Orthodox observance, he was forbidden to use electricity, work, or write. Strangely enough, procreating or the act of was encouraged, but only if the people were married (to each other). Moreover, Jig couldn't conduct any kind of business, even getting me home safely. And since he wasn't permitted to touch money, let alone spend it, guess who hailed her own cab and paid for the ride home?

I mumbled "Shabbat Shalom" to him, the emphasis on Shalom. (As in, goodbye.) It wasn't even nine o'clock when I got home, so I called up an old flame and met him for a quickie. Does that make me a bad Jew?

✡

SECTS AND THE CITY
by GOLDIE LOX

Shabbat Shalom
Week Two

Not one to throw out the baby with the bathwater, I decided to accept a date with another Jewish fella for the next Friday night. Mr. Cig was a conservative Jew who had brown curly hair that I could restyle very easily for him. I met Mr. Cig one night outside the restaurant where he worked as a chef. He lit my after-dinner cigarette and that's when I saw his small Jewish star necklace. I dropped some Yiddish and the next thing I knew he had invited me for Shabbat dinner the next week. I had my concerns. Was this going to be déjà-Jew?

Cig was preparing a Shabbat dinner that he said was going to blow my mind like a shofar on Rosh Hashanah. I liked the sound of that and dressed accordingly in a tube dress. He opened the door to his classic-six apartment and immediately told me that before anything happened, we had to say the blessings first. I said the

prayer over the candles and remembered how my mother had told me how when a woman says these blessings she becomes a momentary priestess. It felt righteous and I was happy to be in the glow of the candlelight. It was not only meaningful but highlighted my new pearly eye shadow. Is that shallow?

"Shabbat Shalom," I purred. This time I meant it in that hel-LO way.

A feast was awaiting us in the form of a brisket, some kugel and other delicious foods that I dared not eat for fear of popping out of my too tight dress. Cig blessed the bread and the wine. He ate, I drank and we both kibbitzed and shared a smoke on his wraparound terrace. He told me about his last girlfriend and I told him about my previous relationship(s). I did my hair twirl and he did the dishes. I could do this every week, no problem. As I thought about what to wear for next week's Shabbat dinner, Mr. Cig suggested that we go out.

"I go to a conservative tem-

ple. We combine the new traditions with the old. And there are a lot of people like us there. You know, lookers," said Cig.

A good-looking congregation appealed me. I felt confident no one would want to drape me in itchy fabric. When we got to the temple, the line was around the block and the people were dressed to the nines. Actually, they were more dressed to the sevens as this wasn't exactly Fashion Avenue. But I knew what Cig meant about lookers. He was getting more handsome by the minute. And it was nice to know he thought I was a looker too. Or did he say hooker?

Evidently Cig's temple had Friday night events where all the lookers gathered. He seemed a bit uncomfortable as he lit up two cigarettes at the same time. That's when he started kvetching about how he doesn't consider me a nice Jewish girl. What am I then?

I asked him what the deal was about asking me out on a date and he told me that it wasn't a date at all. He

thought that we were bot on the prowl, that is "look for dates with other peo other "lookers." Is it kosh be dissed on Shabbat?

I looked away to the cr of people in their knock dresses, sensible shoes, brisket breath. This felt rit istic all right, but it just di feel like Shabbat. I decide go home but not befor bummed a final smoke fr Cig. I wished him well finding his perfect Jew Mrs. Right. I had a fee he'd do just fine as the wom seemed to outnumber the n by at least 4 to 1. As I lit up thought about the earlier p of the evening: the cand and the blessings, the n meal and the welcoming fe ing. I felt warm inside. Or w that the eight glasses of win

Another taxi ride home an ungodly early hour left n with nothing to do on anoth Friday night. So I looked my old Bat Mitzvah pictur that I had hidden in the ba of my closet in a shoebo They made me think abo how some Jewish rituals ca be wonderful and fulfillin They also made me reall thankful I had gotten a nos job and that no one woul ever see these pictures. Th only problem I had now wa what to do next Friday night

SECTS AND THE CITY
by GOLDIE LOX

Shabbat Shalom
Week Three

I spent the week dodging ls from Mr. Jig and Mr. g, who both wanted to see : again for reasons that had thing to do with Shabbat. r. Jig wanted his mother's awl back and Mr. Cig want- to know if I knew anyone ho would want to go to the atzo Ball with him. By iday afternoon I had opped answering my phone d decided to go out for a ocktail. I was beginning to ink that Shabbat wasn't for ie. I needed a drink or five to ally think it over. Who eserved it more?

As I sat on a slippery arstool in a slimy neighbor- ood bar, sipping Mani- chewitz spritzers, I contem- lated my failed experiments nto all things Shabbat. Did I vear the wrong clothes? Why

couldn't I make Shabbat work for me?

"Maybe your expectations are too high," said Swig, a man in too tight jeans and white sneakers. Either this Mr. Swig had read my mind or I had spoken out loud again.

"Tough day? Must be if you're drinking that swill," he said.

"It reminds me of being Jewish. I'm trying to 'do Shabbat,'" I explained, using finger quotes to get my point across to him. Would he think that was cute?

"I was raised as a Reform Jew, which meant that we went to synagogue twice a year, prayed mostly in English and celebrated Shabbat by chilling out."

I told him how I spent the last two Shabbats in a Orthodox shul and on the periphery of a Conservative singles event. I also told him

that the most fun I had was blessing the candles, eating the meal, and drinking the wine.

Mr. Swig smiled and told me that if that's how I wanted to spend Shabbat, then it was kosher by him. Shabbat after all is a time to replenish your mind, body, and soul.

"We can also celebrate Shabbat at happy hour down the block if you want," he said.

Swig paid for my drink while I decided I could use some refreshment, too. So we got a corner booth and refreshed ourselves until it was nearing 2 a.m. The hang- over was already starting and I figured it was time to leave. I got out my taxicab money by rote. I went to say goodnight to Swig but he was passed out. Would I always be destined to go home alone?

On the way out I whispered

"Shalom" into his ear. It was- n't hello and it wasn't good- bye. I wished him peace. He was going to need it if only for his hangover. I hobbled to a cab and thought about how Swig had ignited a powerful idea in me. If I wanted to cel- ebrate Shabbat so badly but didn't like the rules of each denomination, why not make up new rules?

As I stumbled into bed I thought about my plans for the next Friday night. I would invite three of my women friends over for some chilled bottles of Manischewitz on the rocks. We would bless the candles together. I thought about how fab we would all look in the candlelight! We would celebrate Shabbat with- out compromising fashion or taste, or by setting women's liberation back forty years. After all, who needs Jig, Cig, or Swig when you've got sup- portive women friends, catered food, and, of course, new shoes to show off?

Also, afterwards we could always go out and get trashed.

✡ ✡ ✡

CIRCUMCISION

CIRCUMCISION is done on newborn Jewish male babies. There are lots of spiritual reasons why it's done besides "it looks neater than not," but if you ask most people they will tell you that "it looks neater than not" (no disrespect to the uncut). The ins and outs of Circumcision are shady at best — there's a special man to do the cutting (yes, this is his actual job), people picked to hold the child during the ceremony (they're still "thanking" you for that) and a lot of deli meats for afterwards (hopefully the good stuff). Truthfully it all makes sense if you just get schooled on the whole process. And who better to do just that than animated fruit?

ten

Circumcision

Anyway, you slice it.

Circumcision

For Boys

Color 'n' Learn!

It is written in the Torah…

"On the eighth day, you shall circumcise the flesh of his foreskin."

CIRCUMCISION is necessary because as long as the foreskin is present, the light of G-d will not be drawn to the child. It's believed that only through circumcision can this inherent connection be revealed. Without circumcision, the Jew's inherent connection to G-d will remain hidden!

What's a bris, anyway?

A bris is a Jewish birth ceremony during which a baby boy is brought into the covenant of the Jewish people. The ceremony includes a little showstopper called circumcision.

What's the "point" of a bris?

Parents link their son to thousands of years of Jewish heritage. (Start singing "Tradition" from *Fiddler on the Roof* here.)

What's a mohel?

The mohel (it rhymes with boil) officiates at the bris and performs the actual circumcision. He or she is an expert (don't ask what he/she practices on) and has been trained in a hospital setting. He/she also knows the Jewish laws inside and out. He's/she's not a rabbi, but he/she plays one on TV.

What happens at the bris?

A bris usually takes about 15 to 20 minutes. The mother lights candles, and then the baby is brought into the room on a pillow. He is placed on the Chair of Elijah, and the Mohel explains this symbolizes the prayer that the baby grow up in a world of peace and righteousness. The actual incision then occurs, after which the baby is given his Jewish name.

So you want to get circumcised, but it's waaay past your eighth day on earth? You can still do it, and it'll count retroactively! It's impossible to bring a Jewish soul back to life, but circumcision can serve to clarify the nature of the previous situation. (Hurts like all get-out though!)

Does circumcision hurt the baby?

People once believed that a baby wasn't aware enough to feel pain. We now know that's a load of shmutz. Measurements of heart rate and blood pressure during the procedure, plus the shrill screaming and facial grimaces, indicate that babies experience intense pain. The ritual may only last for a matter of seconds, but a baby cannot be considered a willing participant. Then again, they won't remember any of this!

What if he won't stop screaming?

Don't worry! Babies heal very quickly, and minimal care is usually needed after the circumcision, since babies tend to heal quickly. Just keep the area covered with a Vaseline-lubricated gauze pad and apply Bacitracin for a few days. There, all better now.

As a guest, will I have to do anything?
(Translated: Do I have to look?)

An honor called a *kvater* (*kvaterin* for a female) is bestowed upon the godparents of the baby. The kvater gets to place the baby on the Chair of Elijah. The highest honor is the *sandek*—this is the person who actually holds the baby during the circumcision. Another sandek holds the baby while he receives his name.

What happens next?

The bris concludes with gargantuan amounts of food being served. Might I suggest hefty amounts of alcohol, as well?

"I'm not a Super Jew," says Barbara Rushkoff (originally Barbara Kligman), "I don't go to services. But I'm Jewish and it's a part of my identity." A researcher and journalist, Rushkoff started her Jewish-themed zine, Plotz, in 1995 after a co-worker asked her why she didn't want her desk decorated at Christmastime. While she ended the zine in 2001 to work on her writing full-time you can visit her on the web at www.plotzworld.com.

This is her first book.

Photo by Loren Mindak

Appreciation and gratitude to the people who make me kvell: my steadfast agent Daniel Mandel, designer extraordinaire and fontiest man in the land, Sean Tejaratchi, artists Jack Pollock and Mindy Sparango for their wonderfully cheeky illustrations, lady-editor Kathleen Jayes for being gentle with the editing pencil, my mother Jane Kligman for passing down the word "fachadded" to me and my husband Douglas Rushkoff who made this book, and everything in general, a whole lot better.